Pop S

A Musical for Teens

Book and Lyrics by
Peter Morris

Music by
Ben Morss

A SAMUEL FRENCH ACTING EDITION

SAMUELFRENCH.COM

ISBN   978-0-573-63042-2   Printed   in   U.S.A.   #17855

MUSIC USE NOTE

Licensees are solely responsible for obtaining formal written permission from copyright owners to use copyrighted music in the performance of this play and are strongly cautioned to do so. If no such permission is obtained by the licensee, then the licensee must use only original music that the licensee owns and controls. Licensees are solely responsible and liable for all music clearances and shall indemnify the copyright owners of the play and their licensing agent, Samuel French, Inc., against any costs, expenses, losses and liabilities arising from the use of music by licensees.

IMPORTANT BILLING AND CREDIT
REQUIREMENTS

All producers of *POP STAR must* give credit to the Author of the Play in all programs distributed in connection with performances of the Play, and in all instances in which the title of the Play appears for the purposes of advertising, publicizing or otherwise exploiting the Play and/ or a production. The name of the Author *must* appear on a separate line on which no other name appears, immediately following the title and *must* appear in size of type not less than fifty percent of the size of the title type.

Pop Star

Book and Lyrics by
Peter Morris

Music by
Ben Morss

was originally produced in April 2003 by the
Teen Theatre of the Jewish Community Center of Manhattan
in partnership with the Anti-Defamation League.

The company included:

Christopher Alvaro	Eliana Lane
Joseph Amelar	Rachel Lin
Candice Aming	Akilah Lovell
John Barbera	Angela Locantore
Jeremy Cohen	Christine Locantore
Janette Fernandez	Jessica Macauda
Julia Friedman	Rachel Mann
Ariel Gros-Werter	Rebecca Newman
Karl Josef Co	David Periera
Dean Kronfeld	Sarah Rapaport
Emily Vigoda Kurland	Jen Wachs
Carlie Lambert	

Directed by Sasha Nanus
Choreographed by Winter Gabriel
Musical Direction by Barbara J. Anselmi

AUTHOR'S NOTE

On one level, *POP STAR* is a fast-paced, funny look at the cultural phenomenon of reality TV shows like *American Idol*. But on a deeper level, it is a musical about cultural diversity and tolerance of those who are different from us. In *POP STAR*, you will find representatives of various ethnicities: Protestant, Jewish, African-American, Italian and Latino. Depending on the make-up of your particular school or theatre company, these ethnicities can be switched from character to character. For example, in the original production Tony became a Chinese-American because the most talented boy available for the role was Chinese-American. The plight of young lovers from different backgrounds still existed and that was all that mattered. Directors should feel free to adjust the character's ethnicities as they see fit so long as they remain true to the basic concept of the show and the realities of the different characters. But most important of all, *POP STAR* is a chance for young people to sing and dance and have a good time doing a musical. We hope you and your audiences enjoy the show.

ABOUT THE SET

POP STAR does not require a set but directors and designers should do all they can to help establish the world of a typical American high school. In the original production, director Sasha Nanus created a school cafeteria environment by having two long tables surrounded by chairs on either side of the stage. Posters like "Denise for Student Council President" and "Drama Club Meeting, Wednesday at 3:30" were hung all about the stage. Whether or not you choose to go this route with your production, try not to overcomplicate the design as cumbersome set pieces and set changes will only slow down the pace of the show.

ABOUT THE COSTUMES

Costumes should be contemporary, colorful and appropriate to the characters. Steven, of course, needs a yarmulke; and B.O. should look as homeboy as possible. If you are short on boys and chose to have the actor playing either Tony or Chris double as Jordan, try to make him look as different as possible in each role by utilizing a wig and glasses.

CHARACTERS

(16 girls, 5 boys)

Bryan Richards, the host of Pop Star, late 20s – early 30s
Steven Glickman, the smartest kid in school
Tony Benotti, the school's leading jock
Chris Malloy, Tony's friend and the school bully
Jordan Bordoni, the latest Pop Star*

Barb McDougall, Bryan's put-upon production assistant, early 20s
Jessica Berk, an all-American girl
Denise Anderson-Bixby, rich and stuck- up
Penny Lowdermilk, Denise's sidekick
Stephie Dellwood, Denise's other sidekick
Chanel Connors, a spunky, no-nonsense African-American girl
Kristal Johnston, Chanel's friend
Linda Palladino, pretty and popular
Nikki Labrusciano, a high-spirited, go-getter with big ideas
Ann Marie Guadelli, Linda & Nikki's friend
Bonnie Orenstein (a/k/a Notorious B.O.), a Jewish rapper
Judy Pringle, a dorky girl in glasses
Melissa Heinritz, a punk rocker with purple hair and Goth-style
     make-up
Marlene Sigorski, a slacker
Tia Hernandez, a rabid Jordan Bordoni fan
Pepper Ortiz, Tia's friend, also mad about Jordan

*Can be played by same actor playing Tony or Chris

MUSICAL NUMBERS

KISS ME LIKE CRAZY	*Jordan*
THE GREATEST THING	*Full Company*
DIFF'RENT	*Steven, Melissa, Judy, Marlene & B.O.*
STICK TOGETHER NOW	*Jessica, Steven, Nikki, Anne Marie, Linda, Judy, Denise, Stephie, Penny, Tia, Pepper, Chanel, Kristal & Marlene*
ONLY IN FAIRY TALES	*Tony & Chanel*
YES, BRYAN	*Barb*
KISS ME LIKE CRAZY (Reprise)	*Tia & Pepper*
THAT'S CHANUKKAH	*B.O., Melissa, Tony & Chris*
NEVER GONNA CRY	*Chanel*
I'M JUST A DIVA	*Denise, Penny & Stephie*
THE GIRL IN THE MIRROR	*Jessica*
DANCE!	*Linda & Company*
THE PRESSURE IS ON	*`Full Company*
DIFF'RENT (Reprise)	*Judy & Steven*
ONLY IN FAIRY TALES (Reprise)	*Tony & Chanel*
THE GREATEST THING (Reprise)	*Full Company*
YES BRYAN (Reprise)	*Barb & Melissa*
BRYAN'S FAREWELL	*Bryan*
I'M JUST A DIVA (Reprise)	*Denise*
STICK TOGETHER NOW (Reprise)	*Full Company*

PERFORMED WITHOUT INTERMISSION

(LIGHTS UP. A banner reading Pop Star *hangs on the back wall of the stage. Standing stage center is JORDAN, a young man with big rock-star hair and sunglasses. He sings:)*

JORDAN.
KISS ME LIKE CRAZY.
KISS ME AS NIGHT FADES INTO DAY.
I ALWAYS DREAMED
SOMEONE WOULD KISS ME JUST THAT WAY.

KISS ME LIKE CRAZY.
I WANT YOUR LIPS PRESSED CLOSE TO MINE.
DON'T EVER STOP.
YOUR KISS INTOXICATES LIKE WINE.

(Thunderous applause and screams. JORDAN bows and exits as BRYAN RICHARDS, a slick and smarmy TV personality, joins him.)

BRYAN. Thank you, ladies and gentlemen, that concludes this week's episode of *Pop Star.* I'm sure all the people at Pleasant Valley High are pretty darn proud of favorite son Jordan Bordoni. *(More thunderous applause.)* Jordan's first single, "Kiss Me Like Crazy," hits stores tomorrow! As for us, we'll be taking our cameras to yet another typical American high school where a panel of typical American high school students will select one of their peers to become the next fabulous, fantastic Pop Star. And that school is ... *(BARB, Bryan's harried and overworked production assistant, enters, carrying a large fishbowl. BRYAN sticks his hand in and pulls out a piece of paper which he reads out loud:)* West Haven High School in West Haven, New Jersey!

(JESSICA, a pretty, all-American-looking girl, runs on stage as

BRYAN & BARB exit.)

JESSICA. West Haven!

(CHANEL, a vivacious African-American girl, runs on stage.)

CHANEL. West Haven!

(DENISE, who can best be described as a snooty W.A.S.P., runs on stage.)

DENISE. West Haven!

(Entire CAST runs on. The Pop Star *banner is removed revealing a large calendar page that reads "Monday, November 13th".)*

ALL. *Pop Star* is coming to West Haven!

(ALL cheer. MUSIC.)

NIKKI & ANNE MARIE.
SCHOOL! SCHOOL!
SCHOOL BELL IS RINGING.
AND EV'RYONE IS HURRYING TO GET TO THEIR CLASSES.
TONY & CHRIS.
RUSH! RUSH!
RUSH THROUGH THE HALLWAY.
FALL INTO LINE WITH THE HUDDLED MASSES.
NIKKI & ANNE MARIE.
HUDDLED MASSES!

STEPHIE & PENNY.
SCHOOL! SCHOOL!
SCHOOL DAY IS STARTING.
FROM 8 TO 3 WE CONCENTRATE ON READING AND WRITING.
NIKKI & ANNE MARIE.
BUT!
TONY & CHRIS.
BUT!
SEXTET.
BUT WHEN IT'S OVER.

THIS DAY OF SCHOOL'S GONNA GET EXCITING.
  OTHER STUDENTS.
REAL EXCITING.

  ALL.
SO EXCITING!
POP STAR BRINGING CAMERAS TO WEST HAVEN HIGH.
NEXT SATURDAY WE'LL BE LIVE ON TV.
POP STAR PUTTING US IN THE NATIONAL EYE.
THIS COULD BE THE GREATEST THING
THAT EVER HAPPENED TO ME.

  JUDY. *(Crossing to JESSICA.)* Hey, Jessica, are you auditioning for *Pop Star*?
  JESSICA. I plan to.
  JUDY. Well, you're a cinch to make the finals. I mean, who's got a better voice than you?
  JESSICA. Thanks, Judy, I appreciate that. But there are lots of better singers than me.
  JUDY. Name one.

(NIKKI & ANNE MARIE cross to LINDA.)

  NIKKI. Linda, you're auditioning for *Pop Star*, right?
  ANNE MARIE. You should.
  LINDA. I'm thinkin' about it.
  NIKKI. Don't think, just do it. This is like the chance of a lifetime.
  ANNE MARIE. She's right.
  NIKKI. You get it and you won't have t' sing with that rotten garage band no more.
  LINDA. Planet Mucus isn't rotten, Nikki. Besides, there are lots'a better singers than me.
  NIKKI. Name one.

(PENNY & STEPHIE run to DENISE.)

  PENNY. Denise! Denise! Are you auditioning for *Pop Star*?
  STEPHIE. You have to. Who else better to represent West Haven than you? Student Council President.
  PENNY. Editor of the Yearbook.
  STEPHIE. Homecoming Queen.

PENNY. Most Popular.

STEPHIE. Most Likely to Succeed.

DENISE. *(Full of false modesty.)* Penny, Stephie, please. There are lots of better singers than me. *(Pause.)* That didn't sound very convincing, did it?

(They laugh.)

CHANEL & KRISTAL.
CLIQUES!
TIA & PEPPER.
CLIQUES!
QUARTET.
CLIQUES DRIVE ME CRAZY.
THE SNOBBY GIRLS WITH SWIMMING POOLS ARE TOTALLY
    PHONY.
CHRIS & TONY.
LUNCH! LUNCH!
LUNCH MAKES ME QUEASY.
STAY FAR AWAY FROM THE FRIED BALONEY.
SEXTET.
FRIED BALONEY!

(CHRIS pretends to vomit. STEVEN, a nerdy boy wearing a yarmulke, walks by carrying his books.)

STEVEN. *(Under his breath.)* Real mature.

CHRIS. You say somethin', Beanie Boy?

STEVEN. It's not a beanie. It's a yarmulke.

CHRIS. *(Swiping the yarmulke off STEVEN's head.)* Hey, look at me! I'm a rabbi!

STEVEN. Give that back!

CHRIS. Make me.

TONY. Give it to him, Chris.

CHRIS. Maybe we could use it as a Frisbee?

STEVEN. Don't!

TONY. *(With authority.)* I said, give it to him.

CHRIS. *(Tossing yarmulke at STEVEN.)* Here's your beanie. Oh, and your bobby pin.

(TONY & CHRIS cross to other side of stage. As TONY passes

CHANEL they look at each other furtively.)

STEVEN.
JOCKS! JOCKS! JOCKS ARE A MENACE.
ESPECIALLY IN GYM, THEY'RE ALWAYS CALLING YOU
    SPASTIC.
JUDY & MELISSA.
SCHOOL! SCHOOL!
SCHOOL ISN'T PERFECT.
DAYS LIKE TODAY MAKE IT SEEM FANTASTIC.
    OTHER STUDENTS.
JUST FANTASTIC!

    ALL.
SO FANTASTIC!
POP STAR BRINGING CAMERAS TO WEST HAVEN HIGH.
NEXT SATURDAY WE'LL BE LIVE ON TV.
POP STAR PUTTING US IN THE NATIONAL EYE.
THIS COULD BE THE GREATEST THING
THAT EVER HAPPENED TO ME.

PENNY. Steven Glickman is so weird.
STEPHIE. The weirdest.
DENISE. You'd think an "A" student would be smart enough not to wear that hat.

(They laugh as does JUDY, who laughs a bit too broadly, almost snorting.)

JUDY. That's funny, Denise. Really funny. You are soooo funny.

(DENISE, PENNY & STEPHIE look at JUDY blankly then turn and walk away.)

MARLENE. She's right. That hat is totally bogus.
JESSICA. It's not a hat, Marlene.
MARLENE. But it's like on his head. The dude is just askin' for trouble. What's he tryin' to prove anyway?
JESSICA. *(Uncomfortable.)* I ... I don't know. What does it matter? Why don't people just leave him alone?

MARLENE. Yeah, like that's ever gonna happen.

(ALL freeze as CHANEL & TONY step forward. They sing the following, facing each other from opposite sides of the stage.)

CHANEL & TONY.
SO MANY FEELINGS ARE BOTTLED INSI-IDE,
THEY TELL ME THESE FEELINGS AREN'T ALLOWED.
  JESSICA. *(Stepping forward.)*
SO MANY SECRETS, THERE'S SO MUCH TO HI-IDE.
WISH I HAD THE COURAGE TO BE PROUD.
  CHANEL, TONY & JESSICA.
WISH THAT I COULD SHOUT THE TRUTH OUT LOUD.

(B.O., a Jewish girl affecting a homeboy look, walks toward STEVEN.)

B.O. Yo, Steven! Wha' sup, my homeboy? You be gettin' your groove on for *Pop Star*?
  STEVEN. Speak English, will you, Bonnie?
  B.O. Who you callin' Bonnie?
  STEVEN. You. You're Bonnie Orenstein. You're in my physics class.
  B.O. I ain't no Bonnie Orenstein. From now on, Notorious B.O. is in the house.
  DENISE. She's got notorious B.O. alright.

(DENISE, PENNY & STEPHIE laugh.)

NIKKI.
I'VE GOT A FRENCH TEST.
  ANNE MARIE.
GOTTA READ "TOM SAWYER."
  MELISSA.
MY LOCKER IS BROKEN.
  CHRIS.
THE PRINCIPAL HATES ME.
  STEPHIE.
CAN'T FIND MY GYM SHORTS.
  PENNY.
THE GIRLS' ROOM IS FLOODED.
  CHRIS.
I'M STUCK IN DETENTION.

JUDY.
I'M GETTING A PIMPLE.
   MARLENE.
MY DOG ATE MY HOMEWORK.
   KRISTAL.
I NEED A VACATION.

   GROUP #1.
I'M LATE FOR CLASS!
   GROUP #2
LATE FOR CLASS!
   GROUP #3.
LATE FOR CLASS!

(ALL dance as BRYAN enters followed by BARB who holds a video camera in her hands. She is constantly filming.)

   ALL.
POP STAR BRINGING CAMERAS TO WEST HAVEN HIGH.
NEXT SATURDAY WE'LL BE LIVE ON TV.
POP STAR PUTTING US IN THE NATIONAL EYE.
THIS COULD BE THE GREATEST THING
THAT EVER HAPPENED TO ME.
THIS COULD BE THE GREATEST THING,
HONEST, IT'S THE GREATEST THING,
THE ABSOLUTELY GREATEST THING,
THAT EVER HAPPENED TO ME.

   DENISE. On behalf of the Student Council, I, Denise Anderson-Bixby, President ...
   PENNY & STEPHIE. Yay, Denise!
   DENISE. ... wish to welcome Bryan Richards and the entire crew of *Pop Star* to our school.

(ALL clap and cheer.)

   BRYAN. Thank you, kids. Let me say that it's really great being back in New York.
   BARB. *(Quietly correcting him.)* New Jersey.
   BRYAN. Right. I can already tell there's a whole lotta talent here at West Hartford High.

BARB. West Haven.

BRYAN. Right. This is gonna be a pretty exciting week for all of us but, before we get started, let me introduce you to my production assistant Barb McDougall.

BARB. Uhm ... hi. I'm ....

BRYAN. Thank you, Barb. Barb will be filming all the behind-the-scenes footage we use on *Pop Star*, so smile pretty when she points the camera at you. *(BARB lifts up her camera and ALL give big, artificial smiles with lots of teeth.)* Auditions will be held in the auditorium tomorrow directly after school. All you budding pop stars sign up with Barb. If you're not auditioning, never fear, you may be selected to be one of our three student judges. Those names will be announced at tomorrow morning's assembly. And remember, whether you're a contestant, a judge or just a no-talent loser, the *Pop Star* camera is focused on you! *(ALL give another toothy grin.)* See you tomorrow, kids!

(The following happens simultaneously: TIA & PEPPER cross to BRYAN; JUDY crosses to JESSICA, CHRIS to TONY, KRISTAL to CHANEL, ANNE MARIE & NIKKI to LINDA. ALL others crowd around BARB, except for STEVEN, who stands alone reading a book.)

TIA. Hi.

BRYAN. Hi.

TIA. I'm Tia Hernandez.

PEPPER. And I'm Pepper Ortiz.

TIA. We're big fans of Jordan Bordoni.

PEPPER. The biggest.

TIA. We'd really like to meet him.

BRYAN. You and every other teenage girl on the planet.

(BRYAN turns and walks toward BARB. TIA & PEPPER lapse into animated conversation.)

JUDY. *(To JESSICA.)* I should really be one of those judges. No one's more qualified than I am. I mean, right down to my name. I'd be Judge Judy. How perfect is that!

JESSICA. It takes more than that to be a good judge. You have to be able to be fair and impartial.

JUDY. I'd vote for you.

JESSICA. You'd be a great judge.

(JESSICA & JUDY cross and join the crowd around BARB.)

NIKKI. Linda, you're gonna need someone to promote you. That's where I come in. I'm gonna be your manager. I'm gonna turn you into the greatest pop star ever.

LINDA. Can you do that?

NIKKI. Sure. Anne Marie, you need to make posters and put 'em up all over school. Stuff like "Linda Rocks!" and "Move over, J.Lo! Here comes Linda!" Make about a thousand of 'em.

ANNE MARIE. Are you crazy? I got a social studies test on Wednesday.

NIKKI. Fine, just make five hundred. Come on, Linda, we gotta get you signed up.

(They rush over and join the crowd.)

KRISTAL. So whatta you think?

CHANEL. I think it's a waste of time.

KRISTAL. I'm thinkin' the same thing.

CHANEL. Look at 'em, all pushin' and shovin', thinkin' they got a chance to be on TV.

KRISTAL. It's stupid.

CHANEL. Insane.

KRISTAL. You signin' up?

CHANEL. You bet.

(They cross toward BARB, passing TONY & CHRIS. Again, TONY & CHANEL steal looks at one another.)

CHRIS. Man, that Chanel Connors is a fox.

TONY. *(Snapping at him.)* Shut up, Chris.

CHRIS. What'd I say?

TONY. Nothing. Come on, we'll be late for gym.

(The school bell rings. ALL start to exit. Suddenly CHRIS runs over to STEVEN and gives him a "wedgie." BRYAN & BARB film the incident.)

CHRIS. Wedgie! Wedgie! Wedgie!

(STEVEN screams and drops his book. CHRIS & OTHERS exit laughing.)

BRYAN. Get that?
BARB. Yes, Bryan.
BRYAN. Perfect!

(They exit. MELISSA, JUDY, MARLENE & B.O. watch as STEVEN struggles to adjust his underwear. His contorted movements create a kind of bizarre dance.)

B.O. What are you doing, my brother?
STEVEN. Do I honestly have to explain it to you? *(Sings:)*

WEDGIES, NOOGIES AND SPITBALLS,
THESE ARE JUST A COUPLE OF THE PITFALLS
OF BEING DIFF'RENT.

JUDY. I know what you mean.

STEVEN.
OH OH OH DIFF'RENT.

MELISSA. Although I've never gotten a wedgie.
MARLENE. Wedgies are gnarly.

STEVEN.
GETTING SHOVED IN MY LOCKER
DOESN'T COME AS TOO MUCH OF A SHOCKER
BECAUSE I'M DIFF'RENT.

JUDY. Like me.
MELISSA. Me too.

STEVEN.
OH OH OH DIFF'RENT.

MARLENE. You're not alone, dude.

STEVEN.
EINSTEIN,

MISTER ALBERT EINSTEIN,
EVEN MEN LIKE EINSTEIN
GET THE OCCASIONAL THWACK.
(He thwacks the side of his head to demonstrate.) Ow! *(Sings:)*

EINSTEIN,
   GIRLS.
EINSTEIN! EINSTEIN!
   STEVEN.
THE ONE AND ONLY EINSTEIN,
   GIRLS.
EINSTEIN! EINSTEIN!
   STEVEN.
I BETCHA ALBERT EINSTEIN
HAD A "KICK ME" SIGN STUCK TO HIS BACK.
   TRIO,
ON HIS BACK

   JUDY.
PEOPLE SHOUTING YOU'RE GEEKY.
   STEVEN, MARLENE & B.O.
YOU'RE A GEEK
   MELISSA.
EV'RYBODY THINKING THAT YOU'RE FREAKY.
   ALL.
BECAUSE YOU'RE DIFF'RENT.
OO-WAH-OO
OH OH OH DIFF'RENT.
OO-WAH-OO

   B.O. & MARLENE.
BULLIES LOVE TO HARASS US.
   STEVEN, MELISSA & JUDY.
YES, THEY DO.
   MELISSA.
GOTTA BE THE FUNKY HAIR

                          JUDY.
                       AND GLASSES.

   ALL.
WHICH MAKE US DIFF'RENT.
OO-WAH-OO

OH OH OH DIFF'RENT.
OO-WAH-OO
OH OH OH DIFF'RENT.
OO

TEASING, TAUNTING AND BAITING
CAN'T GO ON FOREVER SO I'M WAITING
TILL THING ARE DIFF'RENT.
OH OH OH DIFF'RENT.
OH OH OH DIFF'RENT.
OH OH OH DIFF'RENT, YEAH!
OH OH

(School bell rings. COMPANY enters. The top calendar is peeled away revealing another page beneath it which reads "Tuesday, November 14th".)

DENISE. *(Reading off a piece of paper.)* The tenth grade bake sale scheduled for this Thursday is postponed until next Monday. Anyone interested in joining the yearbook staff should speak to either me, Stephie Dellwood or Penny Lowdermilk. *(STEPHIE & PENNY wave.)* Due to illness, all of Mrs. Rayburn's algebra classes are cancelled for the rest of the week. *(ALL cheer.)* Now I'd like to turn things over to Bryan Richards and Barb who have some very special announcements.

(DENISE joins the other students as BRYAN enters carrying the fishbowl, followed by BARB and her camera.)

BRYAN. Okay, kids, time to select our panel of student judges. And our first judge is ... *(He pulls out a piece of paper from the bowl.)* Judy Pringle!

(Mild applause as JUDY rushes forward.)

JUDY. Yes! Judge Judy presiding!
BRYAN. And our second judge is ... *(He pulls out another piece of paper.)* Anne Marie Guadelli!

(Applause as ANNE MARIE steps forward.)

NIKKI. Go, Anne Marie!

BRYAN. And our third and final judge is ... *(He pulls out another piece of paper.)* Shlomo Glickman! *(There is total silence.)* Shlomo?

STEVEN. *(Stepping forward.)* I prefer to be called Steven. And I don't want to be a judge.

BRYAN. You mean you want to be a contestant?

STEVEN. No, I mean I don't want to have anything to do with this. *(ALL gasp.)* Pitting kids against each other, it's sadistic and humiliating.

BRYAN. And your point is?

STEVEN. Look, I don't wanna be responsible for crushing someone's hopes and dreams. No one deserves that.

CHRIS. *(In a high-pitched, mocking tone.)* Shlomo! Oh, Shlomo!

(NIKKI, TIA & PEPPER laugh.)

DENISE. What kind of a name is "Shlomo" anyway? It sounds like something out of Dr. Seuss: the Grinch, the Lorax, the Shlomo.

PENNY. Oh, Denise, you are so bad!

STEPHIE. The worst!

(They laugh. STEVEN glares at them.)

STEVEN. *(Seething.)* All right, I'll do it.

(The laughter sticks in their throats. Silence.)

BRYAN. Fine, we have our three judges. Their duties will begin officially at this afternoon's auditions. See you then! Take the fishbowl, Barb.

BARB. Yes, Bryan.

CHANEL. *(To KRISTAL.)* Look at all this white bread. How's a slice of pumpernickel supposed t' get noticed?

KRISTAL. I hear you.

B.O. I can dig it.

(CHANEL & KRISTAL look at B.O. blankly. School bell rings. ALL disperse and mingle. BRYAN thrusts the bowl into BARB's hands and exits. BARB struggles to hold the large bowl and film at the same. MELISSA crosses to her.)

MELISSA. Is that a Canon XL 1S, interchangeable lenses, high-precision optics, full manual control, PCM digital sound?

BARB. Uh … yeah. I think.

MELISSA. Cool. You mind if I follow you around? '

BARB. You wanna follow me around?

MELISSA. Yeah, I'm thinking I might like to go into TV, the production end. My grandfather's in it.

BARB. Really? What does he do?

MELISSA. He ….

BRYAN. *(Off-stage.)* Barb!

BARB. Oh! Sorry. Gotta go.

(BARB runs off.)

DENISE. Judy, how wonderful for you! A judge on *Pop Star*! Isn't that wonderful, Penny?

PENNY. It is! It's wonderful! Isn't it, Stephie?

STEPHIE. Beyond wonderful!

DENISE. I can't think of anyone who deserves it more.

PENNY. Neither can I.

STEPHIE. That goes double for me.

DENISE. Judy, I've been meaning to ask you, do you ski? Because my parents have a little place in Aspen. Penny and Stephie and I go every year during spring break and I was wondering if you wanted to join us.

JUDY. Aspen! Cool!

DENISE. Why don't we discuss it on our way to class?

JUDY. Hey, Denise, do they have hot tubs in Aspen?

DENISE. Hot tubs and hot ski instructors.

(JUDY, DENISE, PENNY & STEPHIE exit laughing. JESSICA & STEVEN are alone.)

JESSICA. Steven, can I talk to you?

STEVEN. Why? You never talked to me before.

JESSICA. Sure I have.

STEVEN. Name one time.

JESSICA. Uh … in the cafeteria. I asked you to pass me a straw.

STEVEN. That was in kindergarten.

JESSICA. *(Trying to appear sincere.)* But I've never forgotten the moment.

STEVEN. Whatta ya want, Jessica?

JESSICA. To talk, that's all.

STEVEN. About what? Physics? Chess club? My new orthotics? I doubt it. And if you think we're gonna have a deep conversation about Britney Spears or hair scrunchies, you're out of luck. Face it, we have nothing in common.

JESSICA. That's not true, Steven. We're more alike than you know.

STEVEN. Am I a cheerleader and nobody told me?

JESSICA. I am not a cheerleader! And I hate Britney Spears! And I wouldn't be caught dead wearing a hair scrunchie! God, you are so hostile.

STEVEN. For ten years, you ignore me completely, like I'm invisible. Now I'm a judge for *Pop Star* and all of a sudden I'm not invisible anymore. All of a sudden you can see the dorky little Jewish kid. Well, you know what? I don't see you. Got it? As far as I'm concerned there is no Jessica Berk.

JESSICA. Berkowitz.

STEVEN. What?

JESSICA. Berkowitz. That's what it was before my parents changed it. I told you we were more alike than you knew.

(Pause.)

STEVEN. No. You're wrong. We're not alike at all. See, I'm not ashamed of who I am.

JESSICA. Neither am I. I'm just not as brave as you are.

STEVEN. Brave?

JESSICA. You have to be to put up with wedgies and spitballs and name calling and still come to school everyday wearing your yarmulke. I couldn't do that. That's why I keep this under my shirt.

(She pulls out a chai.)

STEVEN. It's nice.

JESSICA. It's a chai. It means life.

STEVEN. I know. I'm Beanie Boy, remember?

JESSICA. I found it in this trunk of my grandmother's old things. I wear it all the time.

STEVEN. It's good luck.

JESSICA. Maybe, but I need more than good luck if I'm gonna get on *Pop Star.*

STEVEN. Listen, Jessica ....

JESSICA. No, Steven, you listen to me. This isn't some whim for me like it is for Denise. It's what I wanna do with my life. I already know that. That's why I do all the school plays. That's why I take voice lessons and dance lessons and go to performing arts camp in the summer. This could be my big break.

JESSICA.
I NEED YOUR HELP.
STEVEN.
I'M SURE THAT YOU DO.
JESSICA.
I CAN'T PULL THIS OFF ALONE.
STEVEN.
TOO BAD, YOU'RE ON YOUR OWN.
JESSICA.
GIVE ME YOUR HELP.
STEVEN.
I TOLD YOU I WON'T.

JESSICA.
HOW CAN YOU BE SO UNKIND?
STEVEN, YOU'VE GOTTA CHANGE YOUR MIND.
WE GOTTA STICK TOGETHER NOW.
WE GOTTA STICK TOGETHER NO-O-OW.
OUR BACKGROUNDS ARE THE SAME.
IT WOULD BE A SHAME
TO NOT BE PARTNERS IN THIS GAME.

STEVEN.
YOU WANNA STICK TOGETHER NOW.
YOU WANNA STICK TOGETHER NO-O-OW.
THIS TEAM OF YOU AND ME
ISN'T GONNA BE.
IT'S NOT A POSSIBILITY.

JESSICA. But, Steven ....
STEVEN. "But Steven" what?

(They freeze. LINDA, NIKKI & ANNE MARIE enter.)

LINDA. You gonna vote for me, Anne Marie?

NIKKI. You *gotta* vote for Linda.

ANNE MARIE. I don't *gotta* vote for no one you guys tell me I gotta vote for.

LINDA. Then who you gonna vote for? Not Denise Anderson-Bixby.

NIKKI. She is bad news.

ANNE MARIE. I'm gonna vote for who's ever the best.

NIKKI. Linda's the best. I'm tellin' you that.

LINDA.
I NEED YOUR HELP.
ANNE MARIE.
I'D HELP IF I COULD.
NIKKI.
UP TO YOU TO SAVE THE DAY.
ANNE MARIE.
I CAN'T. THERE'S JUST NO WAY.
LINDA & NIKKI.
GIVE US YOUR HELP.
ANNE MARIE.
I GOTTA BE FAIR.

LINDA & NIKKI,
HOW CAN YOU DENY A FRIEND?
FRIENDSHIP'S WHAT MATTERS IN THE END.
WE GOTTA STICK TOGETHER NOW.
WE GOTTA STICK TOGETHER NO-O-OW.
FOR CLOSE TO SEVEN YEARS
WE'RE LIKE MUSKETEERS
AND JUST LIKE THAT YOU'RE CHANGING GEARS.

ANNE MARIE.
YOU SAY T' STICK TOGETHER NOW.
YOU SAY T' STICK TOGETHER NO-O-OW.
BUT IN THE JUDGE'S CHAIR,
CROSS MY HEART, I SWEAR
I'M GONNA DO THIS FAIR AND SQUARE.

LINDA & NIKKI. *(In unison.)* But, Anne Marie ....
ANNE MARIE. "But Anne Marie" what?

(LINDA, NIKKI & ANNE MARIE freeze. TIA, PEPPER & JUDY enter. PEPPER is listening to a Discman.)

TIA. So you'll do it?
JUDY. I don't know. Denise is gonna take me to Aspen in the spring.
TIA. That's not 'til the spring. Don't you want anything now?
JUDY. *(Eyeing PEPPER.)* Well, I have always wanted a Discman.
TIA. Pepper, give her your Discman.
PEPPER. It was a birthday present!
TIA. You wanna meet Jordan Bordoni or don't you?
PEPPER. *(Begrudgingly.)* Oh, alright.

(PEPPER hands over the Discman to JUDY.)

TIA. Deal?
JUDY. Deal.

JUDY, TIA & PEPPER.
WE'RE GONNA STICK TOGETHER NOW.

(TIA & PEPPER freeze as MARLENE enters.)

MARLENE. Judy, what's happenin'? I've been looking all over for ya.
JUDY. Were you?
MARLENE. I'm like auditioning for *Pop Star*.
JUDY. *(Mocking her.)* Like really?
MARLENE. *(Totally oblivious to the sarcasm.)* Like yeah, and I totally need yer vote, dude.
JUDY. Well, I need a few things myself.
MARLENE. Like what?
JUDY. Like a Gameboy.
MARLENE. You got it, dude.

JUDY & MARLENE.
WE'RE GONNA STICK TOGETHER NO-O-OW.

(MARLENE & JUDY freeze as CHANEL & KRISTAL enter.)

KRISTAL. *(Holding a piece of paper.)* It's a petition to get an African-American student on that panel of judges.
CHANEL. How many signatures you got?
KRISTAL. Including my own?
CHANEL. Yeah.
KRISTAL. One. You gonna sign?
CHANEL. You bet I am.

KRISTAL & CHANEL.
IF OTHER PEOPLE SIGN
ON THE DOTTED LINE
THEN WE MIGHT GET OUR CHANCE TO SHINE.

(DENISE, PENNY & STEPHIE enter. During the following, JUDY should be center stage, flanked by all the people she has promised to help.
On one side of the stage should be JESSICA & STEVEN and on the other LINDA, NIKKI & ANNE MARIE.)

DENISE. Judy!
STEPHIE & PENNY. Hi, Judy!

DENISE, STEPHIE & PENNY.
THANKS FOR YOUR HELP.
MARLENE, PEPPER & TIA
THANKS FOR YOUR HELP.
JUDY.
DON'T MENTION IT, GUYS.

STEVEN & ANNE MARIE.
THE ANSWER IS NO.

DENISE, STEPHIE, PENNY, MARLENE, PEPPER & TIA.
I KNOW YOU KNOW WHAT TO DO.
JESSICA, LINDA & NIKKI.
COME ON, I'M BEGGING YOU.
JUDY.
YOU'VE GOT MY VOTE.

STEVEN & ANNE MARIE.
CAN'T DO WHAT YOU WANT.

DENISE, STEPHIE, PENNY, MARLENE, PEPPER & TIA.
YOU'RE CERTAIN WE'LL WIN?
JESSICA, LINDA & NIKKI.
I'M DOWN ON MY KNEES.
JUDY.
HONEST, EVERYTHING'S ASSURED.
JUDY, STEVEN & ANNE MARIE.
LISTEN, I STAND BEHIND MY WORD.

DENISE, PENNY, STEPHIE,
MARLENE, PEPPER, TIA,
KRISTAL & CHANEL.
WE GOTTA STICK TOGETHER NOW.

JESSICA, LINDA & NIKKI.
WE GOTTA STICK TOGETHER NOW.

ALL *(except STEVEN & ANNE MARIE).*
WE GONNA STICK TOGETHER NO-O-OW.
IF I CAN COUNT ON YOU.
ALL MY DREAMS COME TRUE.
AND I'LL GET EVERYTHING I'M DUE.

DENISE, PENNY, STEPHIE,
MARLENE, PEPPER, TIA,
KRISTAL & CHANEL.
WE GOTTA STICK TOGETHER NOW.

JESSICA, LINDA & NIKKI.
WE GOTTA STICK TOGETHER NOW.

ALL *(except STEVEN & ANNE MARIE).*
WE'RE GONNA STICK TOGETHER NO-O-OW.
I'M MAKING YOU A VOW
'TIL THE FINAL BOW
WE'RE GONNA STICK TOGETHER NOW.
WE'RE GONNA STICK TOGETHER NOW.
WE'RE GONNA STICK TOGETHER NOW.

(School bell rings. ALL exit. CHRIS & TONY enter. It is later that day.)

CHRIS. So then we corner him in the locker room, smash a few dozen eggs in his hair, cover him with shaving cream and hang him off a coat hook by his underpants. Good plan, huh?

TONY. *(Distracted.)* I guess.

CHRIS. You guess? This is a great plan. Best nerd attack ever.

TONY. Don't you think maybe we've tortured Glickman enough?

CHRIS. Excuse me? He's a nerd. He's supposed to be tortured. It's like the natural order of things. Cats go after mice, dogs go after cats and jocks go after nerds. It's God's will.

TONY. You're crazy.

CHRIS. Come on, you know you wanna do it.

TONY. No.

(CHANEL enters and crosses the stage.)

CHRIS. I don't get it? You used to be totally into this stuff. What's gotten into you?

TONY. Nothing. I just don't wanna do it, okay? Now leave me alone.

CHRIS. You're the one who's crazy, man.

(He exits.)

TONY. Chanel, can I talk to you?

CHANEL. No. I don't have time for you, Tony.

TONY. Don't be this way, baby.

CHANEL. Don't you "baby" me. I ain't your baby.

TONY. Come on, Chanel. You know how I feel about you.

CHANEL. Sure, I know. But nobody else does.

TONY. I told you, my father would freak. He's very ... Italian.

CHANEL. What, he got marinara sauce in his veins?

TONY. He just thinks that Italian boys should date Italian girls.

CHANEL. And whatta you think, Tony? Or don't you got a mind of your own?

TONY.
PLEASE TRY TO UNDERSTAND.
THE WORLDS WE LIVE IN ARE VERY DIFF'RENT,

VERY DIFF'RENT,
GALAXIES APART.
IF I WERE IN COMMAND
THEN I COULD PROMISE A HAPPY ENDING,
HAPPY ENDING,
MADE TO TOUCH THE HEART.

ONLY IN FAIRY TALES
HANDSOME PRINCES FIGHT FOR DAMSELS
WE DON'T LIVE IN ONCE UPON A TIME.
BUT HANDSOME PRINCES IN SHINING ARMOR CAN'T LOVE
    YOU.
NOT WITH ALL THEIR HEART AND SOUL LIKE I LOVE YOU.
PLEASE REMEMBER NO MATTER WHAT THAT I LOVE YOU.
I DO.

(CHANEL tries to leave but TONY stops her.)

PLEASE TRY TO UNDERSTAND.
THE SITUATION IS COMPLICATED,
COMPLICATED,
MORE THAN I CAN SAY.
THIS ISN'T WHAT I PLANNED.
I PICTURED US IN A NEW TOMORROW,
NEW TOMORROW,
BETTER THAN TODAY.

TONY.   **CHANEL.**
ONLY IN FAIRY TALES

                                  FAIRY TALES AR'N'T WHAT
                                      I NEED.

HANDSOME PRINCES
FIGHT FOR DAMSELS.

                                  DON'T YOU TELL ME THAT
WE DON'T LIVE IN   WE DON'T LIVE IN
ONCE UPON A TIME.   ONCE UPON A TIME.
BUT HANDSOME PRINCES
IN SHINING ARMOR
CAN'T LOVE YOU.

                                  DON'T TELL ME YOU LOVE
                                      ME.

NOT WITH ALL
THEIR HEART AND SOUL
    LIKE I LOVE YOU.

                        NO, NOT YOUR HEART AND
                            SOUL.

PLEASE REMEMBER NO
    MATTER WHAT THAT I —

CHANEL. *(Holding back tears.)* I gotta go, Tony.

(She runs off.)

TONY. Chanel! *(Sings:)*

NOW AND ALWAYS AND PAST FOREVER I LOVE YOU.
I DO.   \

*(Dejected, TONY exits. BRYAN sneaks on stage carrying a clipboard.
    He is followed by BARB.)*

BRYAN. Did you get that?
BARB. Yes, Bryan.
BRYAN. Good. It's just the kind of footage the network wants.
"Forbidden Love in New Jersey." Very juicy.
BARB. I don't know about this, Bryan. I think ....
BRYAN. You're not supposed to think, Barb. If I wanted a
production assist who thinks I'd've hired a man. Now shut up and get
ready for the auditions.

*(He looks at the papers on his clipboard and pays no attention to
    BARB as she sings the following out to the audience.)*

BARB.
YES, BRYAN.
ANYTHING YOU SAY, BRYAN.
HAPPY TO OBEY, BRYAN.
IF YOU ASK FOR CREAM IN YOUR COFFEE,
THERE'S CREAM IN YOUR COFFEE.
WHATEVER YOU WANT, I DON'T MIND.

BRYAN. Make sure you get plenty of reaction shots. Lots of close-ups of heartbroken losers. Remember, big tears mean big ratings.

(He laughs.)

BARB.
YES, BRYAN.
LAUGHING AT YOUR JOKES, BRYAN.
EGO NEEDING STROKES, BRYAN?
I'LL BE THERE TO SOOTHE AND CARESS YOU,
TO BATHE AND UNDRESS YOU,
AND POWDER YOUR ROSY BEHIND.

'CAUSE I'M YOUR ASSISTANT,
YOUR UNDERPAID ASSISTANT,
READY TO DO WHAT I MUST
FOR A GLAMOROUS TV CAREER.
SINCE I'M YOUR ASSISTANT,
I CAN'T BE TOO RESISTANT.
I HAVE TO DO WHAT YOU TELL ME TO DO
OR I'M OUT ON MY EAR.

BRYAN. I'm going to change. I think I'll wear the blue shirt. It brings out my eyes.
BARB. Should I change?
BRYAN. Sure. Change into someone less pathetic. Like that's possible.

(He exits laughing.)

BARB.
YES, BRYAN.
PUT ME IN MY PLACE, BRYAN
STEPPING ON MY FACE, BRYAN.
YOU CAN'T GIVE ME CONNIPTIONS.
MY PROZAC PRESCRIPTIONS
WILL HELP ME DEAL WITH THE STRESS.
SO YES, BRYAN, YES, BRYAN,
YES, BRYAN, YES, BRYAN,
YES, YES, YES, YES,
YES!

\

(School bell rings. MUSIC. It is later that day.
Students enter carrying a table and three chairs. STEVEN, JUDY &
ANNE MARIE enter and sit at the table with notepads and
pencils. The others enter and gather on the opposite side of the
stage. BRYAN enters and takes center stage.)

BRYAN. All right, guys, you know how this works. Each judge
rates each contestant from one to ten with thirty being a perfect score.
All votes are kept secret until the announcement of the finalists
tomorrow. And now ....

KRISTAL. Wait a minute! I protest. We need an African-
American judge.

BRYAN. I'm sorry, honey. Clarence Thomas just isn't available.

KRISTAL. Don't you patronize me.

CHANEL. Give it to him, girlfriend.

KRISTAL. This is unfair and unconstitutional. And I'm not the
only one who thinks so. I got a petition.

(She hands petition to BRYAN.)

BRYAN. There are only six names on this thing. And one of
them is on it twice.

(KRISTAL takes back the paper, looks at it then shoots a look at
MARLENE.)

MARLENE. Sorry, dude.

(Embarrassed, KRISTAL backs away.)

BRYAN. And now, if there are no further interruptions, *(He*
shoots a look at the students, none move.) let the parade of talent
begin. Please welcome our first contestants ... *(He picks up a*
clipboard from the table.) Tia Hernandez & Pepper Ortiz.

(Applause as TIA & PEPPER come center stage.)

TIA & PEPPER.
KISS ME LIKE CRAZY.
KISS ME AS NIGHT FADES INTO DAY.
I ALWAYS DREAMED

SOMEONE WOULD KISS ME JUST THAT WAY.

KISS ME LIKE CRAZY.
I WANT YOUR LIPS PRESSED CLOSE TO MINE.
DON'T EVER STOP.
YOUR KISS INTOXICATES LIKE WINE.

*(They suddenly stop singing and run straight for the camera, pushing
    each other aside.)*

    TIA. You intoxicate me, Jordan! I love you!
    PEPPER. I love you more! Marry me, Jordan!
    TIA. You? He ain't gonna marry you! He's marryin' me!
    PEPPER. Dream on! He's mine!

*(THEY start to argue as BRYAN rushes over and pushes them away
    from the camera.)*

    BRYAN. Thank you, girls, thank you, but it's time to move on.
(They keep blowing kisses into the camera.) Move on! *(They move.)*
Our next contestant is ... *(Not believing the next name on his
clipboard.)* Notorious B.O.?
    B.O. Chillin' and willin' t' give you some thrillin'. Yo, homies!

*(MELISSA, MARLENE, NICK & TONY put on dark glasses and ski
    caps and join her center stage.)*

    DENISE. This oughta be good. Should I vomit now or later?
    PENNY. Oh, Denise, you are so bad!
    STEPHIE. The worst!

    B.O.
GOTTA A LITTLE STORY AN' THE STORY AIN'T A FIB.
JUDAH AN' THE MACCABEES WAS CHILLIN' IN THEIR CRIB.
THEY GOT THE MATZO,
LOTS AND LOTSA,
AND ON A SLIVER
THEY SPREAD THE LIVER.
THEY HAD IT ALL DELIVERED.
YEAH, THEY WAS LIVIN' LARGE 'TIL THE OIL GOT LOW.
THEY HAD NO EXXON. THEY HAD NOWHERE T' GO.

BUT GOD HE MADE A MIRACLE AND KEPT THE LAMP
ABLAZE.
AND ONE DAY OF OIL LASTED EIGHT WHOLE DAYS.

HOMIES.
THAT'S CHANUKKAH.
B.O.
COME ON! COME ON!
HOMIES.
IT'S CHANUKKAH.
B.O.
COME ON! COME ON!
HOMIES.
CHANUKKAH.
B.O.
YEAH!
HOMIES.
THAT'S CHANUKKAH.
B.O.
YEAH!

HOMIES.
PLAYIN' WITH DREIDEL 'N BUSTIN' A MOVE
WE'RE ALL GETTIN' IN THE CHANUKKAH GROOVE.
NUN, HAY, GIMMEL, SHIN!
B.O.
TAKE IT ALL, PUT ONE IN,
SPIN IT AGIN!

GETTIN' DOWN ON CHANUKKAH, MENORAH CANDLES
    MELT.
FORGET ABOUT THE BENJAMINS,
LIVE LARGE ON CHOCOLATE GELT.
BUT DON'T FORGET THE REASON THE MIRACLE
    OCCURRED.
THE HOMIES PERSECUTION,
THAT'S THE WORD.
SO WHEN YA SPIN YER DREIDEL AND LETTERS START T'
    BLUR.
REMEMBER WHO YOU ARE AND WHERE YOU WERE.
OR I'M-A BUST A CAP, AND I DON'T MEAN A YARMULKE.

AND THAT'S THE STORY, THE STORY OF CHANUKAH.

HOMIES.
THAT'S CHANUKKAH.
   B.O.
COME ON! COME ON!
   HOMIES.
IT'S CHANUKKAH.
   B.O.
COME ON! COME ON!
   HOMIES.
CHANUKKAH.
   B.O.
YEAH!
   HOMIES.
THAT'S CHANUKKAH.
   B.O.
YEAH!

   HOMIES.
PLAYIN' WITH DREIDEL 'N BUSTIN' A MOVE
WE'RE ALL GETTIN' IN THE CHANUKKAH GROOVE.
NUN, HAY, GIMMEL, SHIN!
   B.O.
TAKE IT ALL, PUT ONE IN,
SPIN IT AGIN.

(ALL break dance.)

   HOMIES.
THAT'S CHANUKKAH.
   B.O.
COME ON! COME ON!
   HOMIES.
IT'S CHANUKKAH.
   B.O.
COME ON! COME ON!
   HOMIES.
CHANUKKAH.
   B.O.
YEAH!

HOMIES.
THAT'S CHANUKKAH.
  B.O.
 YEAH!

  HOMIES.
PLAYIN' WITH DREIDEL 'N BUSTIN' A MOVE
WE'RE ALL GETTIN' IN THE CHANUKKAH GROOVE.
NUN, HAY, GIMMEL, SHIN!
  B.O.
TAKE IT ALL, PUT ONE IN,
SPIN IT AGIN.

*(Applause. MUSIC. There is a passage of time suggested by a change
  in the lighting. CHANEL takes center stage.)*

  BRYAN. Contestant Number 9, Chanel Connors.
  B.O. Yo! Rock the house, soul sister!

(CHANEL looks at TONY.)

  CHANEL.
NO MORE ROSES AND MOONLIGHT.
I'VE STOPPED DREAMING ABOUT YOU.
NOW THAT YOU'RE NOT HERE
SORROWS DISAPPEAR.
I'M SO MUCH BETTER WITHOUT YOU.
WON'T START FALLING TO PIECES.
LOOK, MY EYES ARE DRY.
NEVER GONNA CRY

  CHRIS. What's she lookin' at you like that for?
  TONY. For once in your life, Chris, shut up.

  CHANEL.
READY TO MOVE AHEAD AND MAKE A NEW BEGINNING.
READY TO PLAY THE GAME, A GAME THAT I'LL BE
    WINNING.
WON'T GIVE UP UNTIL I STAKE MY CLAIM.
WON'T GIVE UP LIKE SOMEONE I COULD NAME.
READY TO FIND A LOVE, A LOVE THAT WON'T DESERT ME.

READY TO FIND A MAN WHO'D RATHER DIE THAN HURT ME.
I BELIEVE THERE'S SOMEONE WHO'LL BE TRUE.
AND I'M SURE THAT SOMEONE ISN'T YOU.

NO MORE ROSES AND MOONLIGHT.
I'VE STOPPED DREAMING ABOUT YOU.
NOW THAT YOU'RE NOT HERE
SORROWS DISAPPEAR.
I'M SO MUCH BETTER WITHOUT YOU.
WON'T START FALLING TO PIECES.
LOOK, MY EYES ARE DRY.
NEVER GONNA CRY.
NEVER GONNA CRY.
NEVER GONNA CRY.

(*Applause. Again, CHANEL looks over at TONY. This time he turns
away and exits. MUSIC. Another passage of time indicated by a
change in the lighting.*)

BRYAN. Now for Contestant Number 17, Denise Anderson-
Bixby.
DENISE. Denise Anderson-Bixby and the Bixby-ettes.

(*Quickly, PENNY & STEPHIE take their places behind DENISE
where they dance and supply background vocals.*)

NIKKI. Without Denise, they couldn't tie their own shoes.
LINDA. Even with her I think they have trouble.
DENISE. I would like to dedicate this song to all the starving
children of the world. Hit it! (*Sings:*)

EV'RYONE'S GOT A DESTINY.
EV'RYONE'S GOT A DREAM.
EV'RYONE'S ON A QUEST T' BE
SO MUCH MORE THAN THEY SEEM.
EV'RYONE'S GOT A VISION
OF MOUNTAINS THEY MUST CLIMB.

GONNA REACH THAT MOUNTAIN TOP 'CAUSE I'M A DIVA.
BORN TO BE A DIVA.
BORN TO RAISE MY VOICE IN SONG,

UNTIL THE WHOLE WORLD SINGS ALONG,
SING OUT GOOD AND STRONG.
'CAUSE I'M A DIVA,
GOD MADE ME A DIVA,
BLESSED ME WITH A GOLDEN VOICE.
YOU SEE I HAVEN'T GOT A CHOICE.
I MAKE THEIR HEARTS REJOICE.
'CAUSE I'M JUST A DIVA.

CHANEL. Diva. That's a nice way of puttin' it.
KRISTAL. You said it, girl.

DENISE.
EV'RYONE'S GOT A FANTASY.
PENNY & STEPHIE.
YES, THEY DO
DENISE.
SOME OF YOU MAY HAVE TWO.
PENNY & STEPHIE.
OR THREE OR FOUR, OO
DENISE.
EV'RYONE'S GOT A PLAN T' SEE
THEIR FANTASY COME TRUE.
PENNY & STEPHIE.
EV'RYONE'S GOT AN IMAGE
OF GOLD RINGS THEY CAN SEIZE.
GUESS WHO'LL GRAB THE GOLDEN RING 'CAUSE SHE'S
A DIVA!
DENISE.
THAT'S ME!
PENNY & STEPHIE.
BORN TO BE A DIVA!
DENISE.
DIVA!
PENNY & STEPHIE.
BORN TO RAISE HER VOICE IN SONG,
UNTIL THE WHOLE WORLD SINGS ALONG,
SING OUT GOOD AND STRONG.

DENISE.
'CAUSE I'M A DIVA.

PENNY & STEPHIE.
YES, SHE IS!
DENISE.
GOD MADE ME A DIVA.
PENNY & STEPHIE.
YES, HE DID!
DENISE.
BLESSED ME WITH A GOLDEN VOICE.
YOU SEE I HAVEN'T GOT A CHOICE.
I MAKE THEIR HEARTS REJOICE.
'CAUSE I'M JUST A DIVA.

DENISE, PENNY & STEPHIE.
JUST A DIVA,
JUST A DIVA!

BRYAN. *(Stepping forward.)* Number 18, Jessica Berk.
PENNY. Yay, Jessica!
STEPHIE. Yay!
DENISE. What are you doing?
PENNY. I thought we liked her.
STEPHIE. Don't we?
DENISE. Not if she becomes a finalist and we don't.

(JESSICA comes center stage. She looks over at STEVEN who avoids her gaze.)

JESSICA.
ACTRESS IN THE SPOTLIGHT
HAS A PART TO PLAY.
WATCH HER AND APPLAUD HER AT THE END.
WHEN THE SHOW IS OVER
HER MAKE-UP'S WASHED AWAY.
AFTER ALL, IT'S ONLY BEEN PRETEND.
ACTRESS HAS A REAL LIFE,
IT'S REAL AS IT CAN BE.
WISH THAT I COULD SAY THE SAME FOR ME.

THERE'S A GIRL IN THE MIRROR
NO ONE ELSE CAN SEE.
IT'S THE EYES OF A STRANGER.

STARING OUT AT ME.
EVERY TIME WE'RE FACE TO FACE
SHE SEES THROUGH MY DISGUISE.
NO HIDING THE TRUTH FROM THOSE EYES.

ARTIST PAINTS A PICTURE,
HANGS IT ON A HOOK,
HOPES HIS WORK OF ART WILL BRING HIM FAME.
ONLY TWO DIMENSIONS
NO MATTER HOW YOU LOOK.
NO ONE SEE WHAT LIES OUTSIDE THE FRAME.
ARTIST HAS A VISION,
THE VISION SETS HIM FREE.
WISH THAT I COULD SAY THE SAME FOR ME.

THERE'S A GIRL IN THE MIRROR
NO ONE ELSE CAN SEE.
IT'S THE EYES OF A STRANGER.
STARING OUT AT ME.
TRIED FOR YEARS TO FOOL THE GIRL
BUT NOW I REALIZE
NO HIDING THE TRUTH FROM THOSE EYES.

THERE'S A GIRL IN THE MIRROR
WATCHING EVERY DAY.
I CAN SEE HER REFLECTION,
NEVER TURNS AWAY.
WHO SHE IS I'D LIKE TO KNOW
SHE SEEMS SO VERY WISE.
NO HIDING THE TRUTH FROM THOSE EYES.
NO HIDING THE TRUTH FROM THOSE EYES.

(Applause. Again, JESSICA looks to STEVEN for support and approval. Again, he avoids her gaze. She steps aside as BRYAN comes forward.)

BRYAN. And our last contestant … Linda Palladino.
NIKKI. Go, Linda! That's your Pop Star right there! You show 'em, Linda! Whoa!
PENNY. Loud, isn't she?
STEPHIE. Very.

DENISE. They're all like that. Haven't you seen "The Sopranos"?

(They laugh. LINDA crosses to stage center.)

LINDA.
WHEN YOUR WORLD IS TURNIN' WAY TOO FAST.
WHEN YOU'RE THINKIN' THAT YOU JUST CAN'T LAST.
WHEN YOU'RE MIXED UP AND HAVEN'T A CLUE.
WHEN YOU'RE SINKIN' AND YOU'RE IN DISTRESS.
NO ONE ANSWERIN' YOUR S.O.S.
LET ME TELL YOU WHAT YOU GOTTA DO.
DANCE! LET THE MUSIC TAKE YOU.
DANCE! LET THE MUSIC SHAKE YOU.
DANCE! LET THE MUSIC MAKE YOU FLY!

WHEN YOUR FRIENDS HAVE UP AND LEFT YOU FLAT.
WHEN YOUR SAVINGS DISAPPEAR LIKE THAT.
WHEN YOU'RE DOWN TO THE END OF YOUR ROPE.
WHEN THE UNIVERSE IS NEAR COLLAPSE.
WHEN YOU ROLL THE DICE AND YOU ROLL CRAPS.
THERE IS SOMETHING THAT HELPS YOU TO COPE.
DANCE! LET THE MUSIC TAKE YOU.
DANCE! LET THE MUSIC SHAKE YOU.
DANCE! LET THE MUSIC MAKE YOU FLY!

DANCE! FEEL YOUR BODY MOVIN'.
DANCE! RHYTHM'S GOTCHA GROOVIN'.
DANCE! THINGS BEGIN IMPROVIN' WHEN YOU DANCE!

(ALL dance. BRYAN confers with the three judges. At the end of the number, BRYAN steps forward.)

BRYAN. And the finalists are ... *(ALL freeze in anticipation.)* Jessica Berk *(Cheers.)* Linda Palladino *(Cheers.)* Chanel Connors *(Cheers.)* Denise Anderson-Bixby.
PENNY & STEPHIE. And the Bixby-ettes!

(They squeal. General commotion brought on by excitement and disappointment. School bell rings. A new calendar page is revealed reading "Wednesday, November 15ᵗʰ". The students form small conversational groups. BRYAN & BARB stand to one

side. BARB, as usual, is filming.)

NIKKI, KRISTAL, CHRIS, TONY, MELISSA & B.O.
PULSE RATES ARE STEADILY RISING.
THE TENSION IS HARDLY SURPRISING.
EVERYONE TRIES TO PLAY IT COOL BUT THE WAY THEY FEEL
THERE'S NO WAY OF DISGUISING.
ALL THE KIDS, IN A MATTER OF SPEAKING,
ARE STRESSED OUT AND TOTALLY FREAKING.
NO RELAXING.
NOW THE PRESSURE IS ON.

NIKKI. Linda, I've got this big campaign planned for you.
LINDA. What kinda campaign?
NIKKI. I'm thinkin' a gettin' one of those Good Year blimps to fly over the school blinkin' "Linda! Linda! Linda!" in electric lights. Whatta ya think?
LINDA. I think maybe we need two blimps.
NIKKI. *(Excited.)* Yeah!
B.O. *(Crossing to CHANEL & KRISTAL.)* Yo, Chanel, I'm down witch you bein' a finalist.
CHANEL. Thanks, Bon ... uh, Notorious B.O.
B.O. Word!

(She moves on to another group.)

KRISTAL. You think she thinks she's black?
CHANEL. I'm not sure.

(MARLENE, PEPPER & TIA have surrounded JUDY.)

PEPPER. I gave you my portable CD player!
MARLENE. And a Gameboy!
TIA. Yeah, whatta ya say about that, Judy?
JUDY. Uhm ... thanks.

STEVEN, ANNE MARIE & JUDY.
FRIENDSHIPS ARE STARTING TO CRUMBLE
AS LOSERS ARE STARTING TO GRUMBLE.
MARLENE, PEPPER & TIA.
WINNERS ARE ACTING ALL ALOOF BUT IT JUST LOOKS FAKE

WHEN THEY TRY TO BE HUMBLE.
MUST ADMIT YOU'RE INCREDIBLY LUCKY.
    DENISE, PENNY & STEPHIE.
OR MAYBE YOUR SINGING IS SUCKY.
    ALL.
BETTER WATCH IT!
NOW THE PRESSURE IS ON.

    JESSICA. Steven, I just wanted to say thank you.
    STEVEN. For what?
    JESSICA. Well, you obviously gave me a high score.
    STEVEN. I gave you the score your performance deserved. I did
that for everyone, no matter what I personally thought about them.

(DENISE, PENNY & STEPHIE approach them.)

    DENISE. Good morning, Steven.
    PENNY & STEPHIE. Morning.
    ALL THREE. *(In unison, but with an edge.)* Hello, Jessica.

(JESSICA is about to respond but they turn their backs on her.)

    DENISE. Steven, my parents are throwing a little pre-*Pop Star*
victory party on Friday night. Shrimp cocktail, glazed ham, the works.
I do hope you can come.
    STEVEN. I can't. Sabbath.
    DENISE. Well, bring her with you. Yoo hoo, Anne Marie!

*(DENISE, PENNY & STEPHIE turn as LINDA & CHANEL enter. The
finalists eye one another.)*

    LINDA. Jessica.
    JESSICA. Linda.
    DENISE. Chanel.
    CHANEL. Denise.

(They move on. DENISE, PENNY & STEPHIE corner ANNE MARIE.)

    BRYAN.
THIS WILL BE THE SHOW THAT DEFINES MY CAREER,
MAKING ME THE KING OF TELEVISION.

I MAY END UP WINNING AN EMMY THIS YEAR.
THE TRUTH IS NO ONE DESERVES IT,
LET'S FACE IT, NO ONE DESERVES IT,
THERE'S NO ONE WHO DESERVES IT MORE THAN ME.

> **BARB.** *(Correcting him.)* Uhm … "I".
> **BRYAN.** What?
> **BARB.** It's "more than *I*".
> **BRYAN.** I'm on television, Barb. I don't have to be literal.
> **BARB.** Liter*ate*.

(He glares at her, turns and walks away.)

> **CHRIS.** You were really good yesterday, Chanel.
> **CHANEL.** Thanks. Chris. What did you think, Tony?
> **TONY.** I think … *(Overcome with emotion.)* I think I gotta get to gym.

(He exits quickly.)

> **CHRIS.** Yo, Tony! Wait up!

(CHRIS exits as MELISSA crosses to BARB.)

> **MELISSA.** Hey, Barb, can I ask you a few more questions about being a P.A?
> **BARB.** Trust me, Melissa, you don't wanna be a P.A. on *Pop Star*. Bryan will squash you like a bug. You don't wanna end up a yucky mess on the bottom of his shoe, do you?
> **MELISSA.** Oh, I'm not worried about Bryan. My grandfather says ….
> **BARB.** Your grandfather? He can't do anything about Bryan.
> **MELISSA.** Sure he can. He's head of the network.
> **BARB.** *(Stunned.)* He … head of the network?
> **MELISSA.** Now, whatta you say we talk about getting you out from under Bryan's foot.

(They exit. NIKKI crosses to ANNE MARIE and pulls her away from DENISE, PENNY & STEPHIE.)

> **NIKKI.** What are you doin' talkin' to that snake, Denise

Anderson-Bixby?

ANNE MARIE. Now you're gonna tell me who I can talk to?

NIKKI. This is war, Anne Marie. Don't fraternize with the enemy.

ANNE MARIE. Yeah, like you know what "fraternize" means.

(They glare at each other. MARLENE, TIA & PEPPER cross to BRYAN.)

TIA. Mr. Richards.

PEPPER. We need to talk to you.

BRYAN. I'm sorry, girls. I can't introduce you to Jordan Bordoni.

TIA. No, it's not that.

MARLENE. There's like somethin' you gotta know. Somethin' skokie.

PEPPER. One of your judges is dirty.

MARLENE. Real dirty.

PEPPER. Takin' bribes and everything.

BRYAN. How do you know?

MARLENE, PEPPER & TIA. *(In unison.)* 'Cause we bribed her.

(GIRLS lead BRYAN to JUDY. BRYAN drags JUDY offstage.)

ALL.
RUMORS OF SCANDAL ARE SPREADING.
WHO KNOWS WHERE THE CONTEST IS HEADING.
PEOPLE ARE GETTING REALLY MEAN AND THEY JUST
DON'T CARE ON WHOSE FEELINGS THEIR TREADING.
I'VE GOT A SENSE OF FOREBODING
THE SCHOOL'S ON THE VERGE OF EXPLODING.
RUN FOR COVER!
NOW THE PRESSURE IS,
NOW THE PRESSURE IS ON.

(School bell rings. ALL exit but STEVEN. JUDY enters carrying a Discman and a Gameboy. She is upset and walks right past STEVEN.)

STEVEN. Judy.

JUDY. I don't have time. Principal says I have to give these things back.

STEVEN. Why'd you do it?

JUDY. I don't know. Got carried away, I guess. Denise was gonna take me to Aspen. We were gonna sit in a hot tub. Now I have to sit in detention for two weeks.

STEVEN. Sitting in detention seems a lot less painful to me than sitting in a hot tub with Denise, Penny and Stephie.

JUDY. *(Imitating PENNY & STEPHIE.)* Oh, Steven, you are so bad.

STEVEN. *(Joining in the imitation.)* The worst.

(They laugh like PENNY & STEPHIE. Pause.)

JUDY. I'm so ashamed.

STEVEN. Everybody makes mistakes. But not everyone can admit it. You're ahead of most people.

JUDY.
SOMEDAY,
HOPING MAYBE SOMEDAY,
THERE WILL BE A SOMEDAY,
A DAY I WON'T LIVE TO REGRET.

(LINDA & NIKKI enter. They see JUDY, shake their heads and walk past her. CHRIS enters as they exit.)

JUDY.
SOMEDAY,
I'M DREAMING OF THE SOMEDAY,
THE DISTANT, FAR OFF SOMEDAY
WHEN EVERYONE STARTS TO FORGET.

CHRIS. I wouldn't hold my breath. You're gonna be in detention for the rest of your life, Pringle.

STEVEN. Then at least you'll have company.

CHRIS. Ha ha, you're real funny, Beanie Boy. Let's see how funny you are after I pants you.

(He moves toward STEVEN.)

JUDY. Stay away from him, Chris!

CHRIS. Make me!

STEVEN. I can handle this, Judy.
CHRIS. *(Continuing his advance.)* I doubt it.
STEVEN. You better watch it, Chris, or ...
CHRIS. Or what?
STEVEN. Or I'm gonna get medieval all over your sorry behind.

(And with that, STEVEN assumes a martial arts position. He begins waving his arms around, punctuating each movement with the kind of sounds one hears in bad marital arts film.)

CHRIS. You expect me to believe you know some sort of marital arts?
STEVEN. Sure. Haven't you ever heard of "jew-jitsu"?

(Pause as CHRIS contemplates this. Suddenly, he is not so sure of himself.)

STEVEN. What's a matter, Chris? Afraid you can't take me?
CHRIS. *(Apprehensive.)* I ... I could take you ... if I wanted. You're just not worth it.
STEVEN. You're the one who's not worth it, Chris. Now, get out of here before *I* pants *you*.

(They glare at each other, then CHRIS exits.)

JUDY. Whoa, Steven. *(Sings:)*

THAT WAS INCREDIBLY CLEVER.
    STEVEN.
COULDN'T LET HIM PICK ON ME FOREVER.
NOW THINGS ARE DIFF'RENT.
    JUDY.
OH OH OH DIFF'RENT.
    STEVEN & JUDY.
OH OH OH DIFF'RENT.

(STEVEN holds out his hand to her. JUDY takes it. They exit. School bell rings. ALL enter, rushing across the stage. The top calendar page is removed and the new page reads "Thursday, November 16th".)

ALL.
SCHOOL! SCHOOL! SCHOOL BELL IS RINGING.
AND EVERYONE IS HURRYING TO GET TO THEIR CLASSES.

(ALL rush off except for TONY. DENISE, PENNY & STEPHIE on one side of the stage, and CHANEL & KRISTAL on the other.)

DENISE. Tony, are you coming to my party tomorrow night? It's going to be fabulous.
PENNY & STEPHIE. Yes, fabulous.
TONY. Is ... uh ... Chanel coming?
DENISE. Chanel Connors? No, this is a very exclusive affair. Her type wouldn't fit in.
TONY. Whatta you mean by that?
DENISE. I think you know exactly what I mean.
TONY. I think I do and I don't like it. Listen to me, Denise, Chanel is a terrific girl, really terrific, like the most terrific girl there is. No one's more terrific than her. And if she's not welcome at your party then neither am I.
CHANEL. Oh, Tony.

(She runs to him and they kiss.)

DENISE. A white boy and a black girl? That's just not natural.
CHANEL. I'll tell you what's not natural, Denise, the color of your hair.

(PENNY & STEPHIE gasp)

DENISE. Well, that's just rude.

(DENISE, PENNY & STEPHIE exit.)

TONY. I love you, Chanel.
CHANEL. I love you too.

(TONY is about to kiss her again when he notices a grinning KRISTAL hovering over them.)

TONY. Uh, Kristal, do you mind?
KRISTAL. Oh, yeah, sure. You go right on integratin'.

(KRISTAL exits.)

   TONY. I'm sorry I hurt you, Chanel. I promise I'll never let anything come between us again.
   CHANEL. What about your father?
   TONY. If I can stand up to Denise Anderson-Bixby, I can stand up to my father. *(Sings:)*

NOT JUST IN FAIRY TALES
HANDSOME PRINCES FIGHT FOR DAMSELS.
HAPPY ENDINGS HAPPEN ALL THE TIME.
AND HANDSOME PRINCES IN SHINING ARMOR CAN'T
    LOVE YOU.

   CHANEL.
PRETTY DAMSELS IN IV'RY TOWERS CAN'T LOVE YOU.
   BOTH.
NOT WITH ALL OF THEIR HEART AND SOUL LIKE I LOVE
    YOU.
NOW AND ALWAYS AND PAST FOREVER I LOVE YOU.
I DO.

*(School bell rings. ALL enter, rushing across the stage. The old
    calendar page is peeled off revealing one that reads "Friday,
    November 17ᵗʰ".)*

   ALL.
SCHOOL! SCHOOL! SCHOOL DAY IS STARTING.
FROM 8 TO 3 WE CONCENTRATE ON READING AND WRITING.

(ALL rush off except for NIKKI & LINDA.)

   NIKKI. What about the half-time show at the Super Bowl? Five hundred dancers on the fifty yard line spellin' out "Linda" with their bodies. Good, huh? You couldn't lose after that.
   LINDA. But the Super Bowl's two months away. The contest is tomorrow.

(CHANEL & KRISTAL enter.)

   CHANEL. The contest is tomorrow, Kristal.

KRISTAL. There's still time. And this petition is better than the last one. This time I got nine signatures, no duplicates.

(JESSICA enters from one side of the stage. DENISE, PENNY & STEPHIE from the other. There is an awkward moment as all four groups square off.)

DENISE. Well, well, well, if it isn't the competition.

LINDA. Heard you're havin' a victory party tonight. What'd ya win? A dog show?

NIKKI. Ooooo.

DENISE. What are you ooooing at? You couldn't even get into a dog show. You have to be pure breeds for that.

PENNY & STEPHIE. Ooooo.

NIKKI. *(Pointing at DENISE.)* Malocchio! Malocchio!

DENISE. Why are you calling me "Pinocchio"?

NIKKI. Malocchio, not Pinocchio. I'm puttin' the evil eye on you.

KRISTAL. What is that? Some sorta voodoo?

DENISE. Well, you people know all about voodoo, now don't you?

CHANEL. You better watch it, Denise.

DENISE. Or what?

CHANEL. Or I'm gonna snatch you bald-headed.

LINDA. I'd like to see that.

CHANEL. *(Turning on LINDA.)* You think I can't?

LINDA. Get outta my face.

CHANEL. Get outta mine.

JESSICA. Chanel, Linda, everybody, stop it!

(Students gather on stage to watch.)

NIKKI. Listen to little miss goodie two-shoes.

LINDA. Probably thinks we're mutts too.

KRISTAL. Yeah, just 'cause her ancestors landed on Plymouth Rock.

JESSICA. No, they didn't. They landed on Ellis Island.

PENNY. Ellis Island? Where's that?

STEPHIE. I think it's in the Bahamas.

PENNY. I love the Bahamas.

DENISE. Wait a minute? Are you Jewish?

(Pause. JESSICA turns to look at STEVEN, then turns back.)

JESSICA. Yeah. You wanna make something of it?

(ALL begin to argue. Eventually, all join in and the entire stage turns into a riot scene. BRYAN enters followed by BARB with her camera.)

BRYAN. Everybody smile pretty for the camera!

(ALL stop arguing, turn to camera and sing.)

ALL.
POP STAR BRINGING CAMERAS TO WEST HAVEN HIGH.
TOMORROW NIGHT WE'LL BE LIVE ON TV.
POP STAR PUTTING US IN THE NATIONAL EYE.
THIS COULD BE THE GREATEST THING
THAT EVER HAPPENED TO ME.

- *(One by one, the following step forward:)*

DENISE.
ME!
JESSICA.
ME!
LINDA.
ME!
CHANEL.
ME!

(School bell rings. The judges seat themselves at the table as the others arrange themselves as they were for the auditions. The calendar page is peeled away, revealing the final date: "Saturday, November 18th". BRYAN steps forward.)

BRYAN. Okay, people, before we go live we have a little matter to take care of. As you know, one of our judges has been disqualified and needs to be replaced. I've given it a lot of thought and ....
BARB. Hold it.
BRYAN. Who said that?
BARB. Uhm ... I did.
BRYAN. Is the building on fire?

BARB. No.

BRYAN. Then shut up. Now, as I was saying, the new judge ....

BARB. *(Mustering up her courage.)* No. You shut up.

(ALL gasp.)

BRYAN. Are you looking to get fired, Barb?

BARB. You can't fire me.

BRYAN. You're fired if I say you are.

BARB. You better talk to Melissa about that.

BRYAN. Who?

MELISSA. She means me.

BRYAN. What's the purple-headed kid got to do with this?

MELISSA. I see the way you treat Barb and I think it stinks.

BRYAN. *(Sarcastically.)* Do you?

MELISSA. So I told my grandfather.

BRYAN. Oh no, you told your grandpa on me?

MELISSA. And he thinks it stinks too.

BRYAN. Big deal. Why should I care what he thinks?

BARB. You should, Bryan. He's the head of the network.

BRYAN. The head ....

(He is too stunned to finish the sentence.)

MELISSA. My grandfather wasn't happy to hear how you treated your staff. In fact, he hasn't been happy with you for a long time. Turns out your "TVQ" is way down.

B.O. That's wack.

MELISSA. He's been considering replacing you for a long time. This just helped him make up his mind. Barb, if you'd care to do the honors.

BARB. Bryan, you're fired.

BRYAN. You can't fire me.

     BARB.
YES, BRYAN.
YOU ARE OFF THE SHOW, BRYAN.
TIME FOR YOU TO GO, BRYAN.
     MELISSA.
I'VE GOT A NEWS FLASH FOR YOU, SIR.
NOW BARB'S THE PRODUCER.

GRANDDADDY SAYS THAT IT'S SO.

BRYAN. Wait a minute. Give me another chance?
MELISSA. What do you say, Barb?

BARB.
I'VE WAITED SO LONG FOR THIS DAY
NOW I'LL BREAK MY SILENCE AND SAY.
NO, BRYAN,
NO, BRYAN,
NO!

BRYAN. If you fire me now, who's gonna host the show?
BARB. Oh, that's all taken care of.
MELISSA. Yeah, here comes our new host now.

(JORDAN enters.)

TIA. Oh my God!
PEPPER. It's Jordan Bordoni!
TIA & PEPPER. I love you, Jordan!

(They squeal and throw themselves at him.)

JORDAN. Thanks, ladies, but I have some hosting to do.
TIA. Did you hear that? He called me "his lady."
PEPPER. You're crazy. I'm his lady.
TIA. Don't you start in on me.

(As TIA & PEPPER argue, JORDAN gets caught in the middle.)

MELISSA. See, he's got great "TVQ."
BARB. *(Putting the camera in BRYAN's face.)* Let me get a close-up of you, Bryan. Remember, big tears mean big ratings.

BRYAN. *(Pushing camera aside.)*
YOU MAY THINK YOU'VE WON BUT I'M NOT FINISHED YET.
I'LL GO OUT AND GET A TEAM OF LAWYERS.
I WON'T LOSE MY TEMPER. I WON'T GET UPSET.
INSTEAD I'M GONNA GET EVEN
I SWEAR, I'M GONNA GET EVEN

THERE'S NO WAY THAT YOU'LL GET THE BEST OF ME!
(Speaking.) You haven't heard the last of Bryan Richards!

(BRYAN exits. General commotion.)

BARB. Quiet! Quiet! Let's pull ourselves together. We've got a show to do. Now, we need to appoint a new judge. I think, in order to keep things fair and balanced, that our new judge should be Kristal Johnson.

KRISTAL. *(Holding up her petition.)* Power to the people!

(ALL applaud except for DENISE, who scowls.)

BARB. Great. Get ready, kids. We go live in five, four, three, two ....

(MUSIC. BARB lifts camera and points it toward JORDAN.)

JORDAN. Welcome, back. This is Jordan Bordoni, live at West Haven High. Well, it's the moment you've all been waiting for. It's time for the big sing-off where the judges will determine who will be the next Pop Star.

JESSICA. Uhm, Jordan, do we have to?

DENISE. What the matter, Jessica? Turning chicken?

JESSICA. No. It's just that this competition has already caused enough trouble. Look at us: fighting, cheating, conniving. It's not right. I mean, a certain amount of competition is good but this, this is ... how did you describe it, Steven?

STEVEN. Sadistic and humiliating.

JESSICA. Exactly, and I don't wanna be a part of it anymore.

DENISE. So quit and let the rest of us get on with it.

JESSICA. What about you, Chanel? Do you want to get on with it?

CHANEL. No. I don't like the kind of person it's turnin' me into. Linda, I'm sorry I told you to get outta my face. You can get in my face anytime you want.

LINDA. I'm sorry too, Chanel. This whole thing is makin' us crazy.

NIKKI. Oh, Anne Marie, I'm so sorry.

(She runs to ANNE MARIE.)

ANNE MARIE. That's okay, Nikki. I understand. You just got carried away. So did I. I didn't mean what I said. I'm sure you know what fraternizing means.

NIKKI. *(Exploding into tears.)* No, I don't!

DENISE. Look, why don't you all just quit and let me be the new Pop Star.

STEVEN. You're not the new anything until the judges say so, Denise. Right, Jordan?

JORDAN. That's right.

STEVEN. And we're not saying anything. Are we, Kristal?

KRISTAL. No, we're not. We refuse to pick a winner. Right, Anne Marie?

ANNE MARIE. Right. As far as we're concerned, it's a four-way tie.

JORDAN. Is that your final decision?

(STEVEN, KRISTAL & ANNE MARIE shake their heads in unison.)

JORDAN. Well, it's a little unorthodox but if that's what the judges have decided then ....

DENISE. Wait a minute, you mean I don't get to be the winner.

JESSICA. This way we all win, Denise.

LINDA. Yeah, I like that.

CHANEL. So do I.

DENISE. Well, I don't. I should be the only winner

DENISE. *(Sings:)*
'CAUSE I'M A DIVA.
GOD MADE ME A DIVA.
MEANT FOR ME TO STAND ALONE.
THE BRIGHTEST LIGHT THAT'S EVER SHOWN.
DON'T WANNA SHARE THE THRONE
'CAUSE I'M JUST A DIVA,
JUST A DIVA,
JUST A DIVA!

KRISTAL. Have it your own way.

ANNE MARIE. Yeah, do whatever you want.

STEVEN. Penny? Stephie? What about you? You wanna share first place?

PENNY & STEPHIE. Us?

DENISE. Of course they don't. Come on, girls.
PENNY. Um, not so fast, Denise.
STEPHIE. Yeah, not so fast.
PENNY. We don't mind sharing.
STEPHIE. Not at all.
DENISE. Oh really? Then I guess I'm going to Aspen alone this year.

(She starts to exit.)

    PENNY & STEPHIE. Denise, wait!
    DENISE. *(Turning back triumphantly.)* Yes?
    PENNY & STEPHIE. You suck!

(ALL cheer. Humiliated, DENISE exits. PENNY & STEPHIE run to join the other winners. STEVEN crosses to JESSICA and shakes her hand.)

    JORDAN. Here they are, ladies and gentlemen, this week's fabulous, fantastic Pop Stars!

    FINALISTS.
WE'RE GONNA STICK TOGETHER NOW.
WE'RE GONNA STICK TOGETHER NO-O-OW.
IF WE CONSOLIDATE,
THINGS'LL WORK OUT GREAT.
AND WE'LL HAVE CAUSE T' CELEBRATE.

WE'RE GONNA STICK
TOGETHER NOW.
                OTHERS.
                WE GOTTA STICK
                TOGETHER NOW.
    ALL.
WE'RE GONNA STICK TOGETHER NO-O-OW.
I'M MAKING YOU A VOW
'TIL THE FINAL BOW
WE'RE GONNA STICK TOGETHER
WE'RE GONNA STICK TOGETHER
WE'RE GONNA STICK TOGETHER NO-O-OW.

(Blackout.)

          END OF PLAY

PROP LIST

2 or more microphone stands
2 or more microphones*
Fish bowl filled with folded pieces of paper (for Barb)
Video camera (for Barb)
Clipboard (for Bryan)
Notepads (for judges)
Pencils (for judges)
School books (for students)
Book bags (for students)
Discman (for Pepper)
Gameboy (for Marlene)
Sunglasses (for B.O. & Homeboys)
Ski hats (for B.O. & Homeboys)

*The microphones do not have to be practical but if you have a sound system it would be advisable to use them. What's a pop rock score without amplification?

THE HOUSE OF BLUE LEAVES
John Guare

Farce / 4m, 6f / Interior

Artie Shaugnessy is a songwriter with visions of glory. Toiling by day as a zoo-keeper, he suffers in seedy lounges by night, plying his wares at piano bars in Queens, New York where he lives with his wife, Bananas. Artie's downstairs mistress, Bunny Flingus will sleep with him anytime but refuses to cook until they are married. On the day the Pope is making his first visit to the city, Artie's son Ronny goes AWOL from Fort Dix stowing a home made-bomb intended to blow up the Pope in Yankee Stadium. Also arriving is Artie's old school chum, now a successful Hollywood producer, Billy Einhorn with starlet girlfriend in tow, who holds the key to Artie's dreams of getting out of Queens and away from the life he so despises. But like many dreams, this promise of glory evaporates amid the chaos of ordinary lives.

"Enchantingly zany and original farce."
– *The New York Times*

GETTING AND SPENDING
Michael J. Chepiga

Dramatic Comedy / 4m, 3f

A brilliant and beautiful investment banker makes illegal profits of eighteen million dollars from insider trading and uses it to build housing for the homeless. Shortly before her trial, she ferrets out the foremost criminal attorney of the era to persuade him to abandon his retirement in a Kentucky monastery to defend her. This play is about them: their struggles with themselves, with each other, with the law and with her unusual defense.

"Stirs the conscience while entertaining the spirit."
– *Los Angeles Times*

"An off beat, audacious comedy, well worth seeing."
– *WNBC TV*

OTHER TITLES AVAILABLE FROM SAMUEL FRENCH

THE DOWNSIDE
Richard Dresser

Comedy / 6m, 2f / Combined Interior
American business is the target of this hilarious and cutting satire originally produced at Long Wharf Theatre. A pharmaceutical firm has acquired rights to market a European anti stress drug and marketing has got to come up with a snazzy ad campaign. Nowhere is this drug more needed than right here at Mark & Maxwell to counter corporate ineptitude. The strategy meetings get more pointless and frenetic as the deadline approaches. These meetings are chaired by Dave who is never actually there; he is a voice directing the campaign from his mobile phone while jetting between meetings, unstoppable even when his plane is hijacked.

"Funny and ruthlessly cynical."
– *Philadelphia Inquirer*

"Sheer delight."
– *Westport News*